DOODLE
YOUR
DESTINY

DOODLE YOUR DESTINY

DRAW YOUR DREAMS INTO *Reality*

Meera Lester, AUTHOR OF *365 WAYS TO LIVE THE LAW OF ATTRACTION*

Adams media

AVON, MASSACHUSETTS

Published by
Adams Media, a division of F+W Media, Inc.
57 Littlefield Street, Avon, MA 02322. U.S.A.
www.adamsmedia.com

ISBN 10: 1-4405-8651-9
ISBN 13: 978-1-4405-8651-4

Printed in the United States of America.

10 9 8 7 6 5 4 3 2 1

Cover design by Frank Rivera and Elisabeth Lariviere.
Cover illustrations by Elisabeth Lariviere and © iStockphoto.com/
Kalistratova/Shlapak_Liliya.
Interior illustrations by Elisabeth Lariviere.

This book is available at quantity discounts for bulk purchases.
For information, please call 1-800-289-0963.

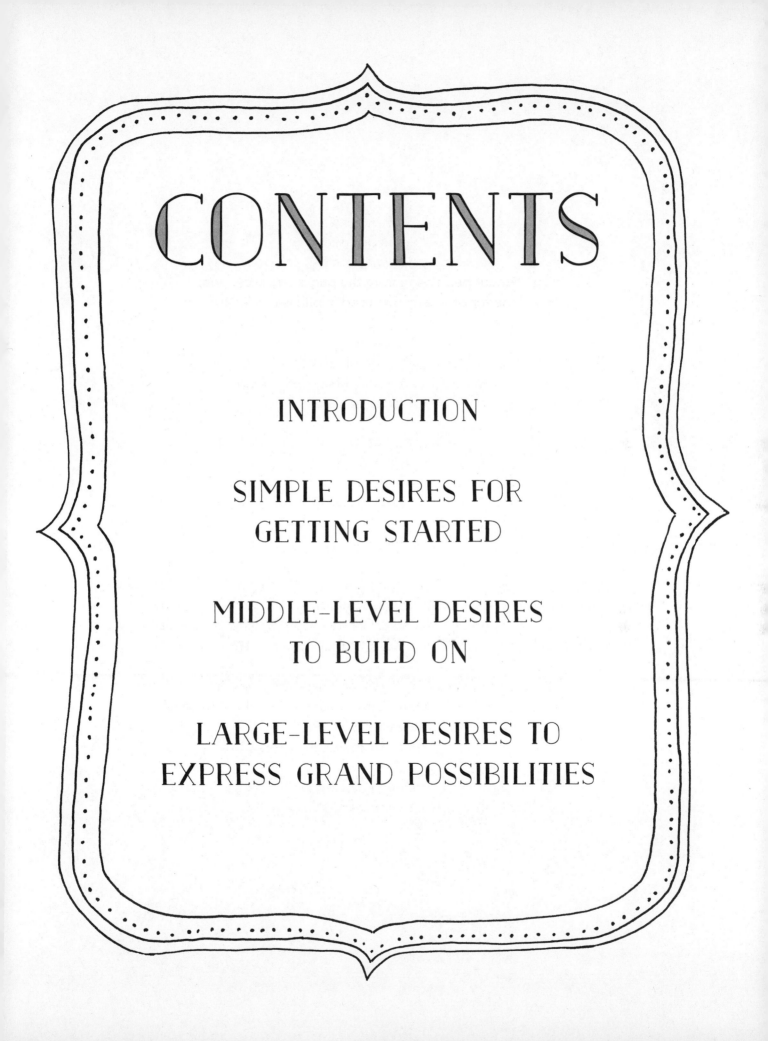

CONTENTS

Introduction

If you could summon a genie who could grant your every wish, what would you desire to draw into your life? You would not be alone if you said more money, a new car, a better house, robust or restored health, an ideal life partner, a happy and healthy family, an exciting vacation, deeper spirituality, a secure job, or an easier track to a challenging career. For many people, these common desires are symbols of a successful life.

Successful people understand how to get what they want. They start with focusing their thoughts on a specific goal they want to achieve. They remain enthusiastic, generating positive energy around their idea, using mind power and willpower to stay on track. Their thoughts, words, and actions are in harmony with accomplishing their intended desire. They build on their success with other successes by remaining focused, fearless, and ever optimistic. Failure, if it occurs, is almost always viewed as a positive; a lesson learned, not to be repeated. They know that optimism is the engine that powers success and that every desire, from the smallest to the largest, begins as a seminal thought that shapes reality.

The Right Mindset Will Serve You

Attitude is everything. Your success in every endeavor in life is accelerated or thwarted by your positive or negative thoughts and habits. By using your creative mind to visualize and fantasize about your desires, you can decide to concretize them or release them like fleeting dreams or wishes. But the desire you hold in your mind and set into intention aligns with a corresponding unseen power that helps it become reality.

Your vision of your successful life begins with choice. Choice can lead to action, mindful living, spiritual pursuit, or public service. If you want it all, you can have it all.

You Are the Genie

You don't have to summon the genie, because you already are the creator of your life. Your thoughts, positive and negative, are attracting to you people, objects, and circumstances, whether or not you are aware of what is occurring. Why not make a conscious choice to attract more of what you desire and less of what you don't?

The process is simple:

- **Start creating your destiny, consciously from where you are in this moment.** Understand that your future is based on desires and choices you make in the present moment.
- **Choose something you want to manifest.** Be clear about your desire. Declare your intention to have that object. Set aside skepticism; believe the object is already on its way to you. Don't try to control the how and when and don't doubt, or you'll attract not having what you want. Work with the unseen forces by initiating action toward your desire.
- **Imagine you are receiving your desire.** Engage in positive thoughts, affirming words, and inspired actions to further solidify your intention of manifesting your desire. Cultivate a joyful, expectant, and grateful state of mind and do not concern yourself with how or when the result manifests. The force that created the universe has unlimited and incalculable organizing power and can handle the details.

The entries in this book are organized into three groups of desires: simple, medium, and large. Consider starting with a simple desire and, as you achieve success, try attracting something more challenging.

Remember, all things great start small, perhaps with a seminal idea . . . and a doodle or two.

SIMPLE DESIRES FOR GETTING STARTED

Make a rough sketch of a clothing item you've always wanted and fully imagine the shape, fabric, texture, color, and smell. Now open a space in your life for that item to appear and when it does, give thanks to the infinite manifesting power of the universe and wear it with style.

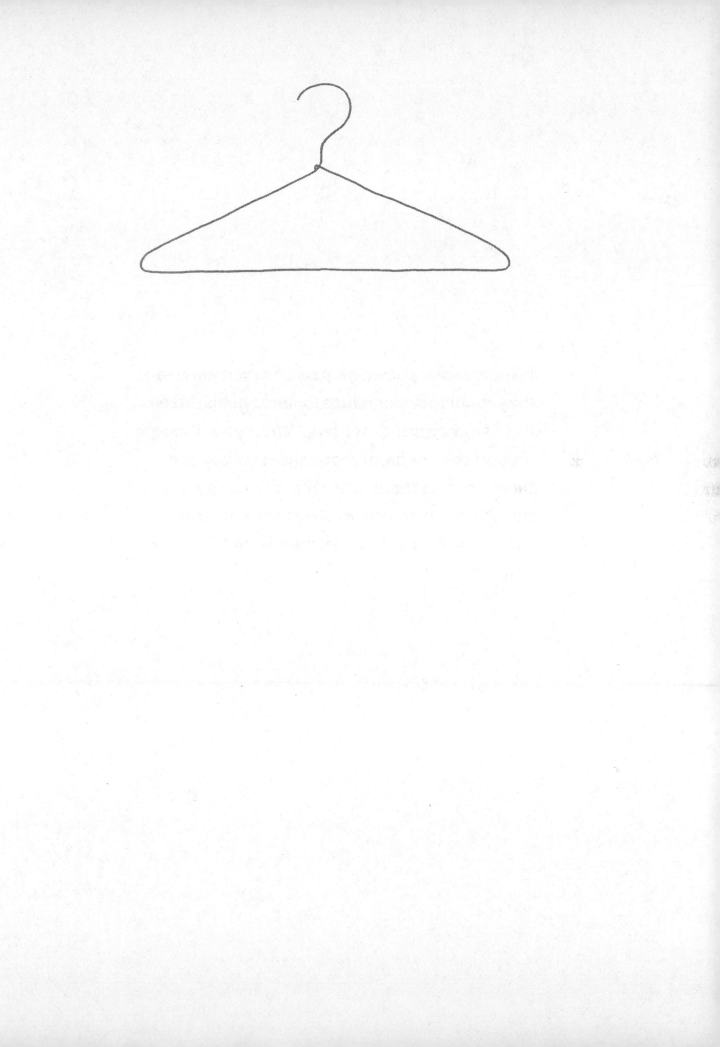

Fill this shoe rack with a pair of new shoes—are they running shoes, clogs, stiletto heels, steel-toed workboots, or waders? Wrap your thoughts around the image of those shoes as you put them on, feel them, marvel at the material, delight in the color and style, enjoy their new scent, and know they are already on their way to you.

Fill in the frame with your new look, starting with the haircut—is it bobbed, brushed back, braided, spiky, curly, or newly colored? Imagine having that new look, hear people complimenting you, notice your rising confidence level, and feel joyful and thankful that by changing your image, you facilitate change in your life.

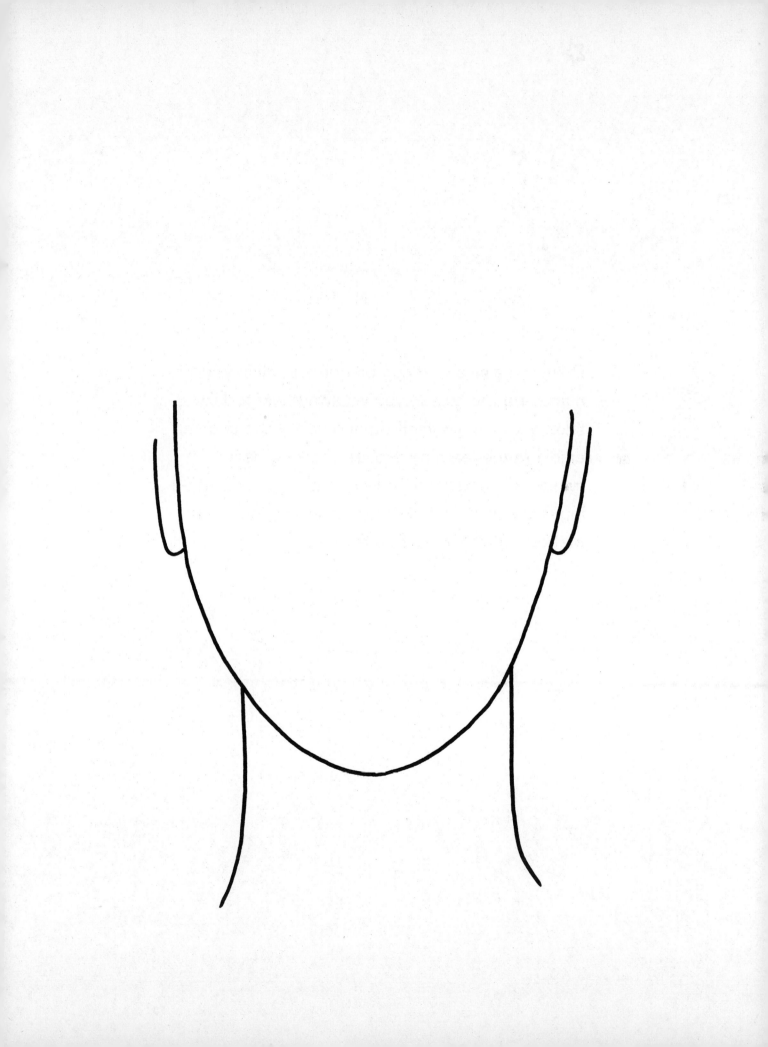

Draw a certificate of completion and fill in your name and the course you've always wanted to take. Visualize yourself signing up for the course, enjoying the learning process, making new friends, sharing what you are learning, and basking in the joy of receiving that certificate of completion with your classmates.

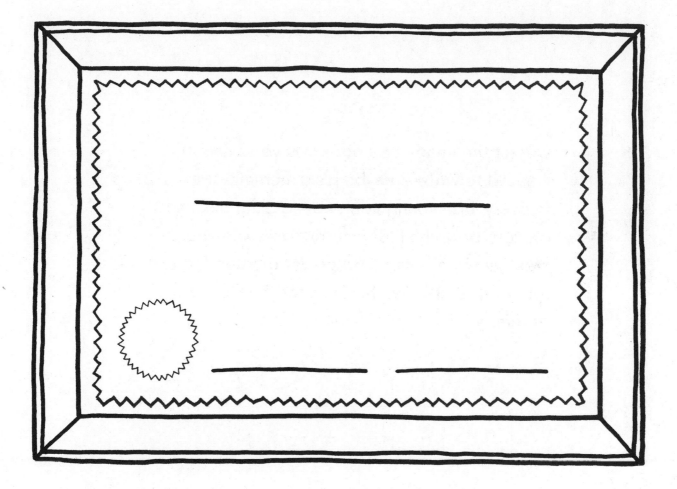

Depict the image of a book you've always wanted to write—maybe it's a memoir, or a mystery, or a young adult novel. Clear a space on your bookshelf for its arrival and use your creative visualization and power of intention to attract it, sharing enthusiasm for the work with others.

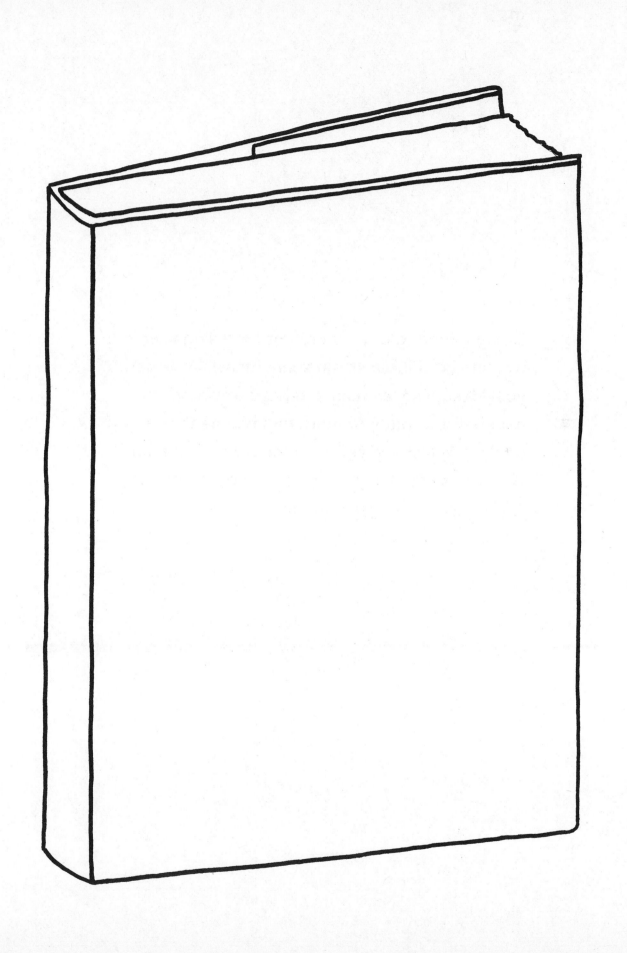

Design the ring of your dreams (perusing jewelry websites or Pinterest can spark ideas). Whether your design style is characterized as vintage, minimalist, ornate, or modern, imagine that ring on your finger and see its color, style, stone, and sparkle as you enjoy wearing it on different occasions and with diverse outfits.

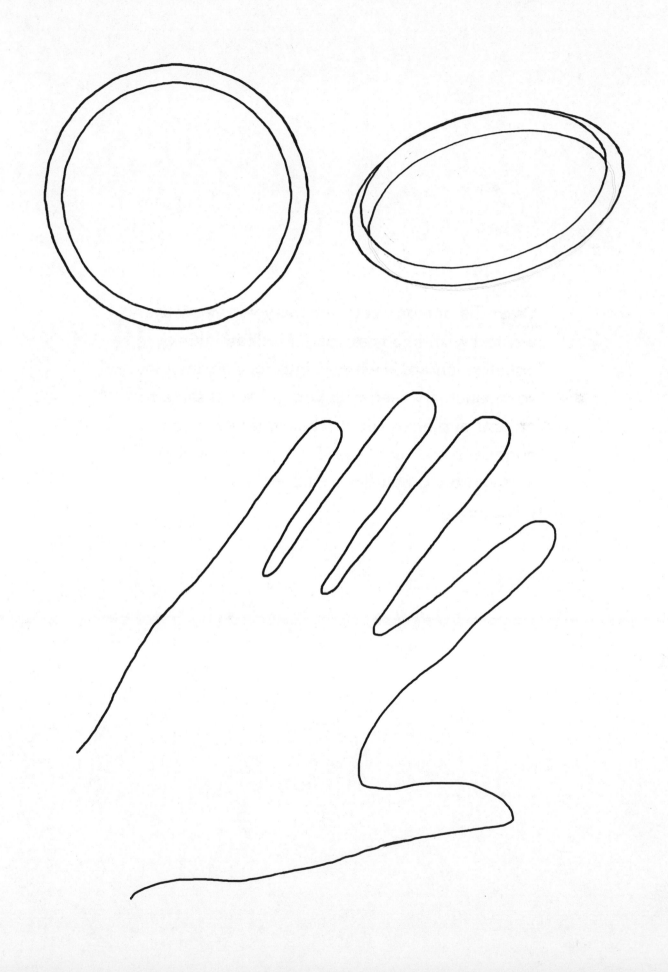

Draw the personalized sanctuary you've always wanted where you can read, meditate, think, visualize, and pray without interruption. Imagine your sanctuary filled with your personal sacred objects and a cushion or chair where you can engage in creative visualization, set intentions, and express gratitude for the manifestations in your life.

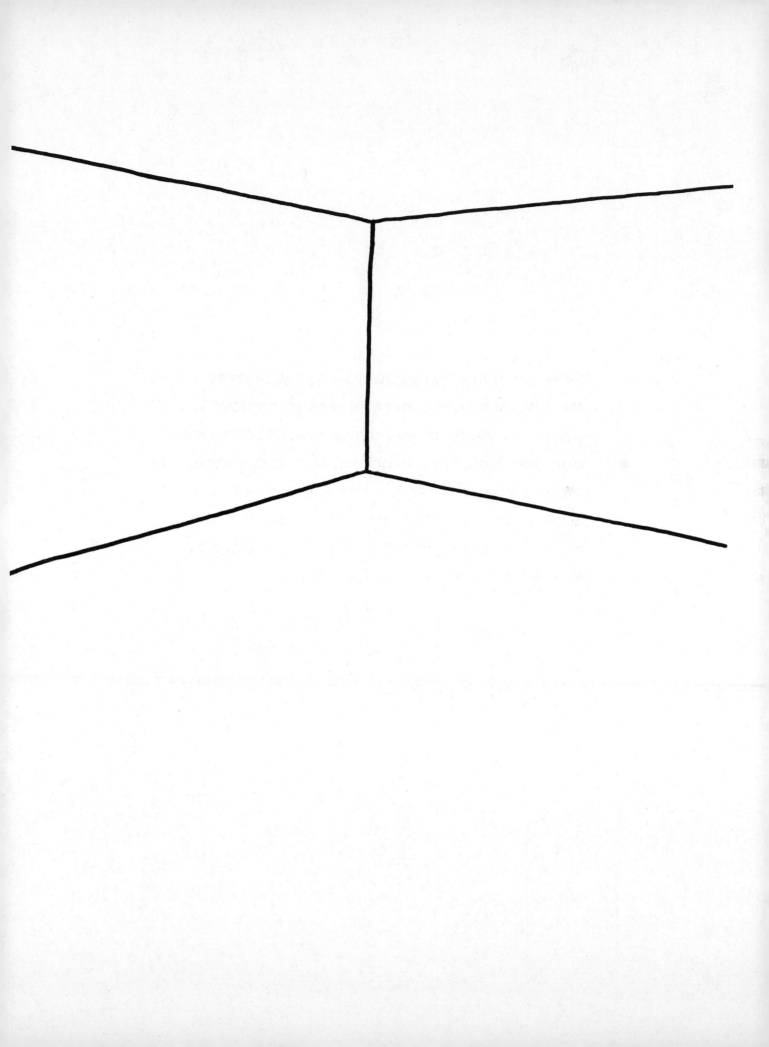

Draw an image representing a talent, such as dancing or singing, that you seek to improve upon and for which you'd love feedback and recognition. Visualize performing a song or dance, make a powerful intention to polish your talent, and—after a friend or family member records your amazing performance—post your video on your website or on social networking sites.

With your mind on your health, find a place in nature where you can move and breathe deeply, knowing your actions will set up a correlation in the field of infinite possibility to manifest excellent health benefits. Now picture yourself outdoors engaging in a physical activity that will cultivate perfect health. Do you want to walk more? Bike farther distances? Practice yoga?

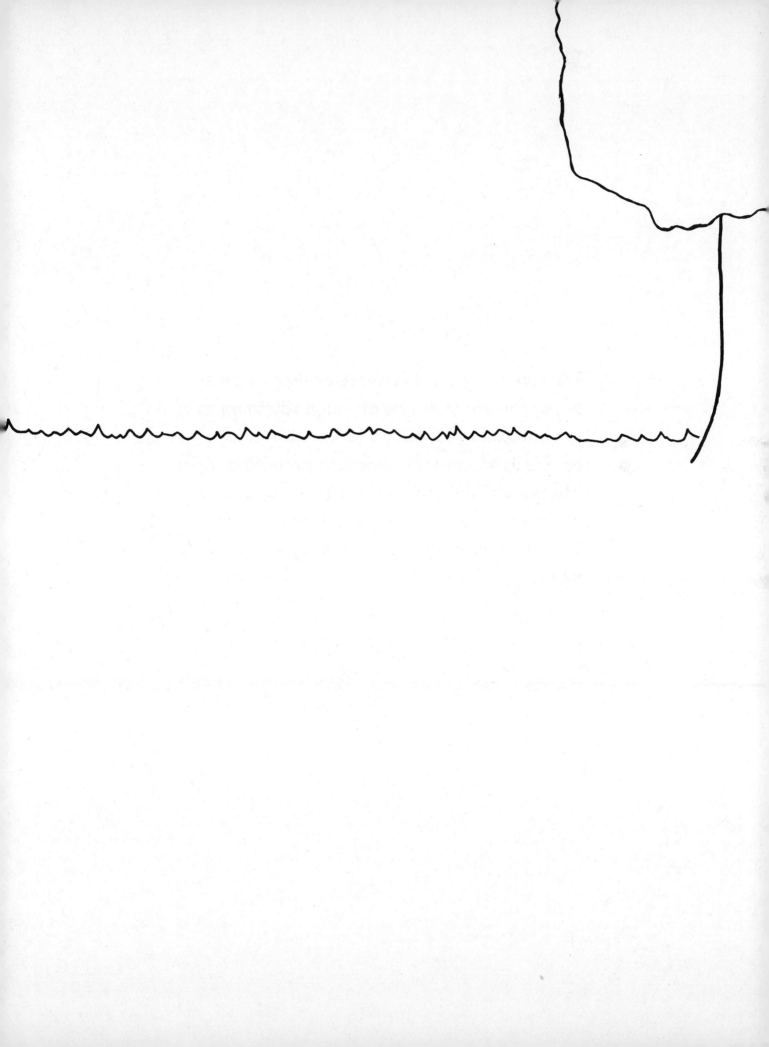

If you are feeling ill and desire healing, draw an "X" on the affected area of your body. Imagine light suffusing your body with warmth to correct, heal, and restore all cells to perfection. Trust your body's ability to heal itself, intend to have complete healing, and know that the restorative power in creation brings you what you deeply desire.

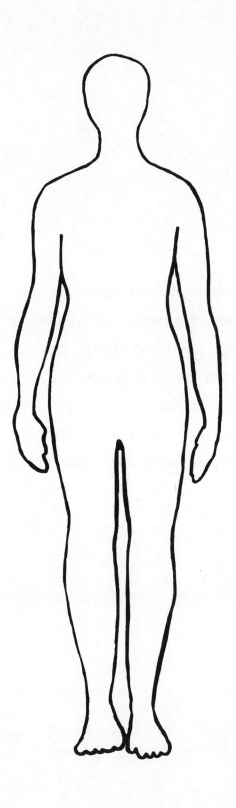

Imagine eating dinner at your favorite restaurant and make a quick doodle of the image. See the service pieces, smell the food, take an imaginary bite and hold it on your tongue to savor the flavor, hear the ambient sounds, feel the texture of the tablecloth and napkins—in short, evoke the full sensual experience as fantasy and then make it happen.

Make time and space for a new, good habit by letting go of a bad habit and sending it into the universe's open hands. Draw the negative habit (e.g., eating junk food, gossiping, having a negative attitude) you are releasing in order to embrace a healthier habit. With your resoluteness, clear thinking, and right action, your success is assured.

Imagine being in the garden of your dreams. This peaceful place is perfect for you to happily have tea with friends or practice your golf swing. Decide how you would like this outdoor space to be laid out. Draw in your favorite types of flowers and plants, design your ideal sitting area, and think about the many things you could do in this wonderful space.

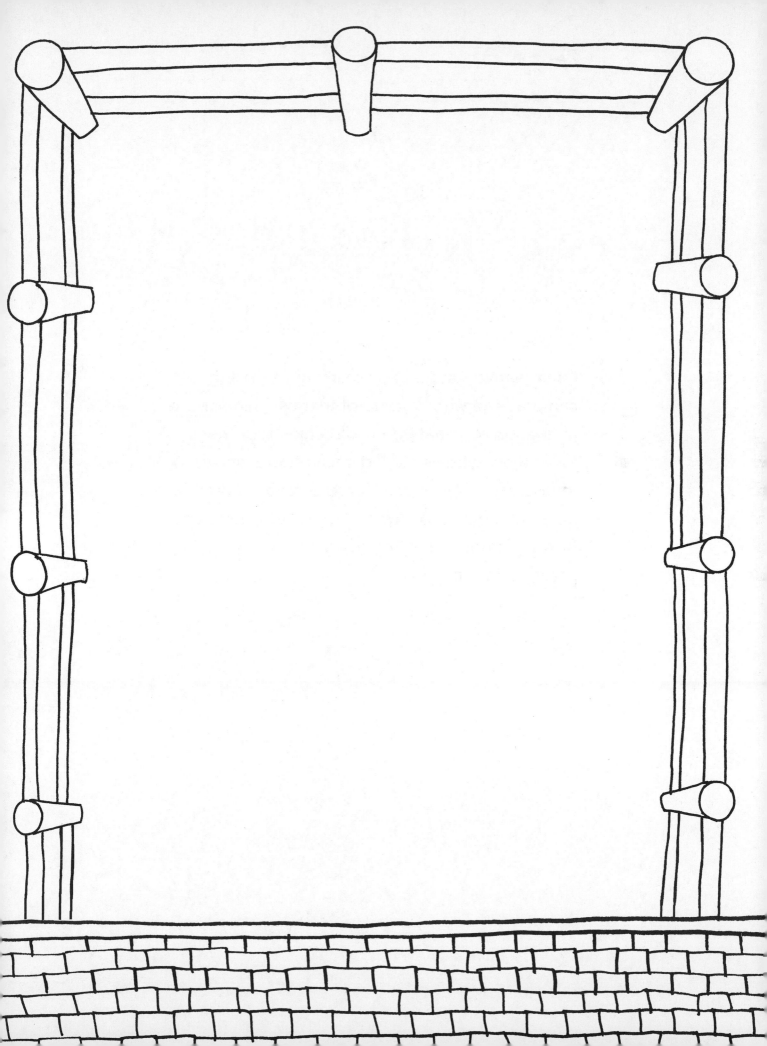

Use creative visualization to imagine sharing camaraderie with a group of friends. Think about all the fun activities you could enjoy together. Picture everyone enjoying each other's company as you organize a group for your favorite outdoor activity. You could draw a playing field, a Frisbee flying through the air, or an area for you all to practice Tai Chi.

Imagine attracting plentiful ideas about how to manifest a healthy, strong physical body animated by an equally strong spiritual vision for a long life. No matter where you're starting from, you can make it happen. Picture yourself working toward that goal.

Regardless of your age or other factors, you don't have to do anything to attain happiness because it is already yours to claim, according to the Buddha's teaching. Find your happiness in each moment and visualize and intend to live in a state of blessed ease and contentment. Sketch a little thing that made you happy today, so that you remember to find happiness in each moment of your day.

Sketch the image of a dog, cat, bird, or fish to symbolize the pet you want to welcome into your life. Imagine finding an animal you bond with after visiting a pet store, animal shelter, or rescue organization. With clarity of mind, declare an intention for having that pet, which you will shower with unrestrained affection for years to come.

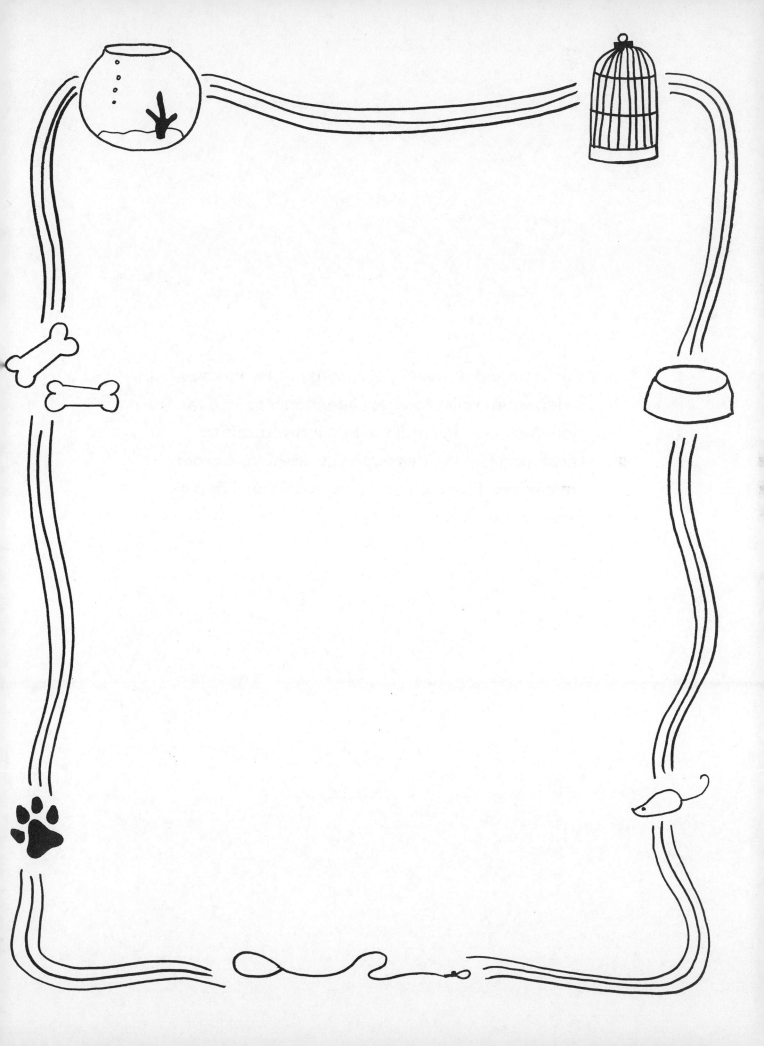

Focus on the all-seeing eye image at bedtime as a departure point to inject intention and inspiration into your dream time. Remind yourself to recall your dream ideas upon awakening in order to manifest them. Illustrate an aspirational dream in order to bring it into reality.

Bring order to your home and regain control of your stuff, whether it's cluttering your office, closet, studio, kitchen, or other area of your life. Get rid of anything you don't need, then visit stores or look online for organization and storage ideas. Visualize making use of them in your cluttered space. Form the intention to manifest control by organizing this disorganized area.

Wind chimes, Tibetan bells, and tabletop water fountains help to establish a harmonious and peaceful ambience in your home. What type of sound do you find calming? Imagine that sound and then what creates it. Draw a picture of that object to help manifest the serene environment it creates.

Write in your ideal weight. Visualize looking into
a mirror and seeing yourself look back with a
smile. Pay close attention to the gleefulness in
your heart for the knowledge that your desire
and intention have resulted in that healthy, newly
sculpted body. Think of the various healthy habits
you can begin in order to reach that ideal weight
and doodle them around the scale.

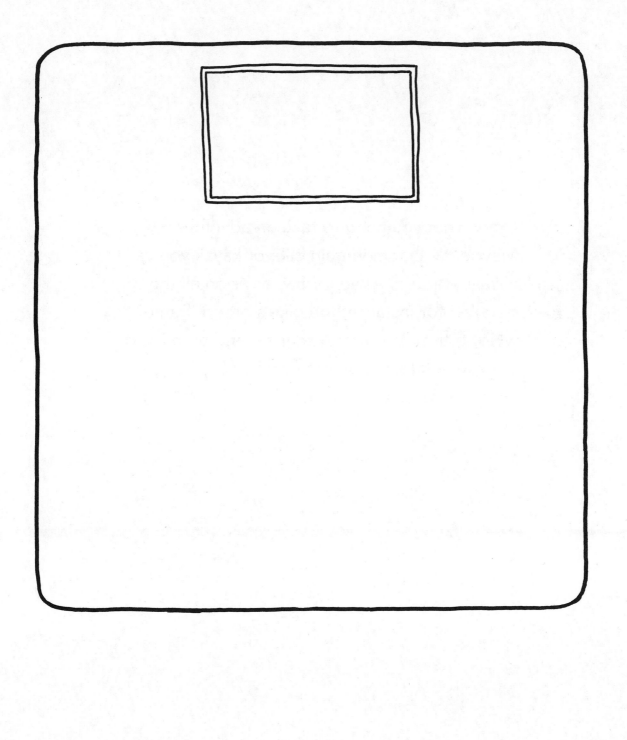

Draw what you need to take an adventure. Maybe it's that mountain bike or kayak you've always wanted. As you draw, envision all the details—for instance, the bike's brand, frame, weight, tires, color, seat shape—and then imagine yourself taking off, heart full of joy.

Running a marathon isn't for everyone, but if it's your dream, then make it happen by doodling a runner crossing the finish line. Hold the image in your mind as you imagine feeling the exhilaration while lacing your running shoes, stretching your legs, following your training regimen, racing alongside other runners, sprinting across the finish, and realizing you've achieved success.

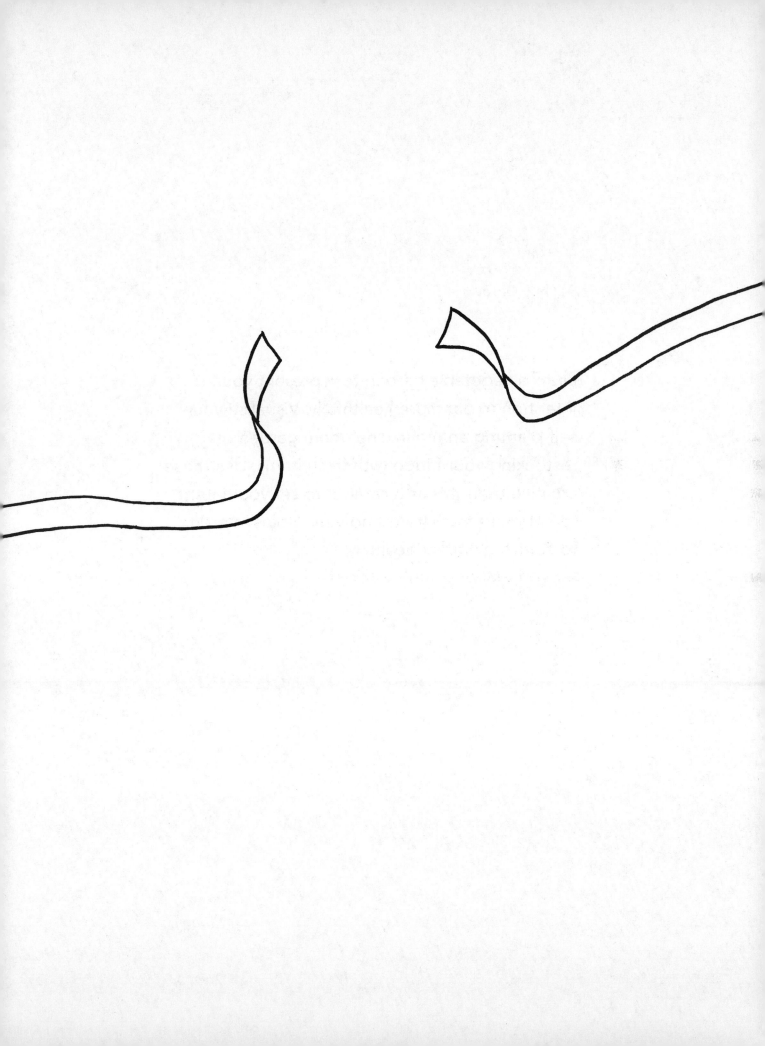

Draw a vegetable garden to represent your intention to eat more healthfully. Visualize yourself planting an organic heirloom garden or restocking your fridge with fresh items. Use those creative thoughts as a catalyst to set your intent to eat more fresh fruits and vegetables in order to cultivate vibrant health.

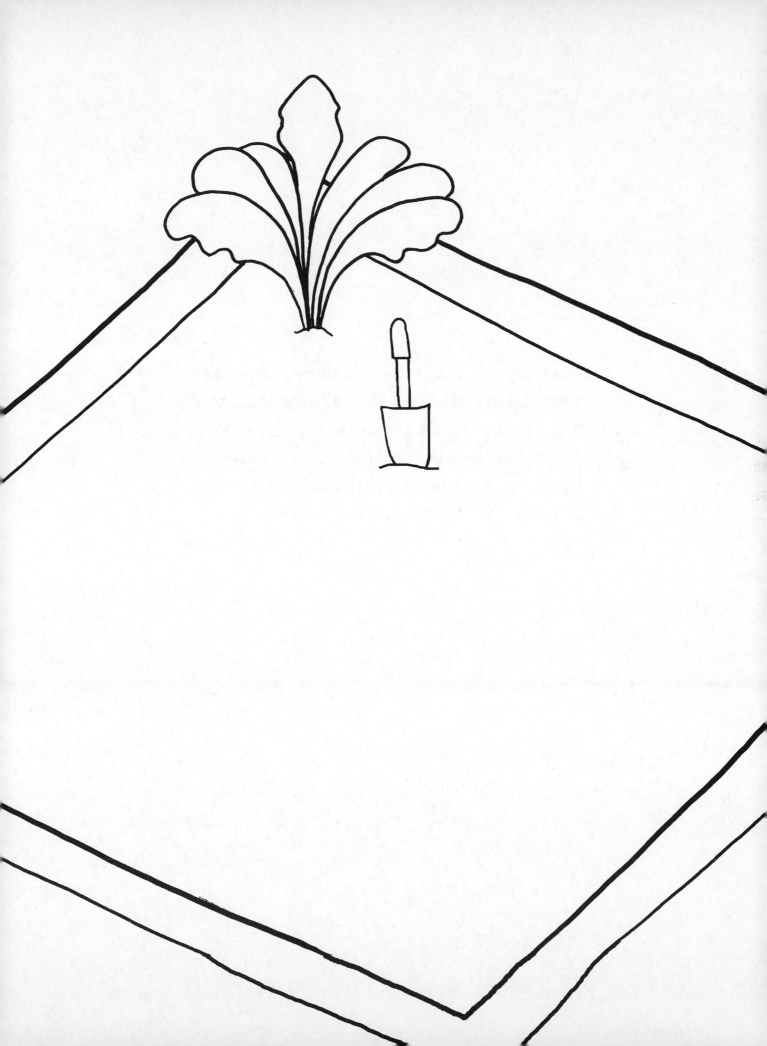

Draw the image of mountain peaks, water, and trees to symbolize your desire to manifest harmony in your family or work environment. Imagine yourself enjoying cooperation with everyone around as you send out harmonious vibes through your thoughts, words, and deeds.

Imagine actually busting your stress with a hammer. In order to manifest a tension-free life, put an imagined end to the most stressful part of it. Draw a picture of what's currently stressing you out and imagine smashing it out of existence. Read a book about relieving stress, sign up for a meditation class, or walk for fifteen to thirty minutes each day (with the intent to gradually increase the time) in order to banish stress.

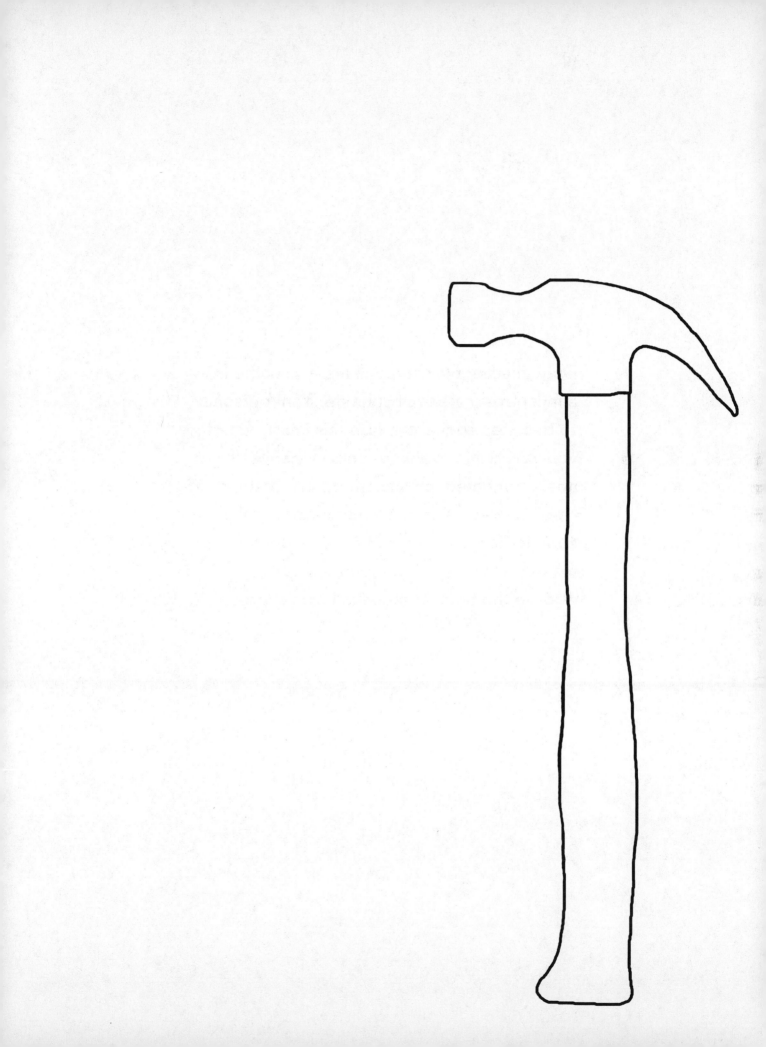

Draw the people you think are invaluable in almost every arena of your life, from personal to business endeavors. Use this image when you would like to ask for help in manifesting a desire for career advancement, a mentor, child-care, love and support, or stronger networking connections.

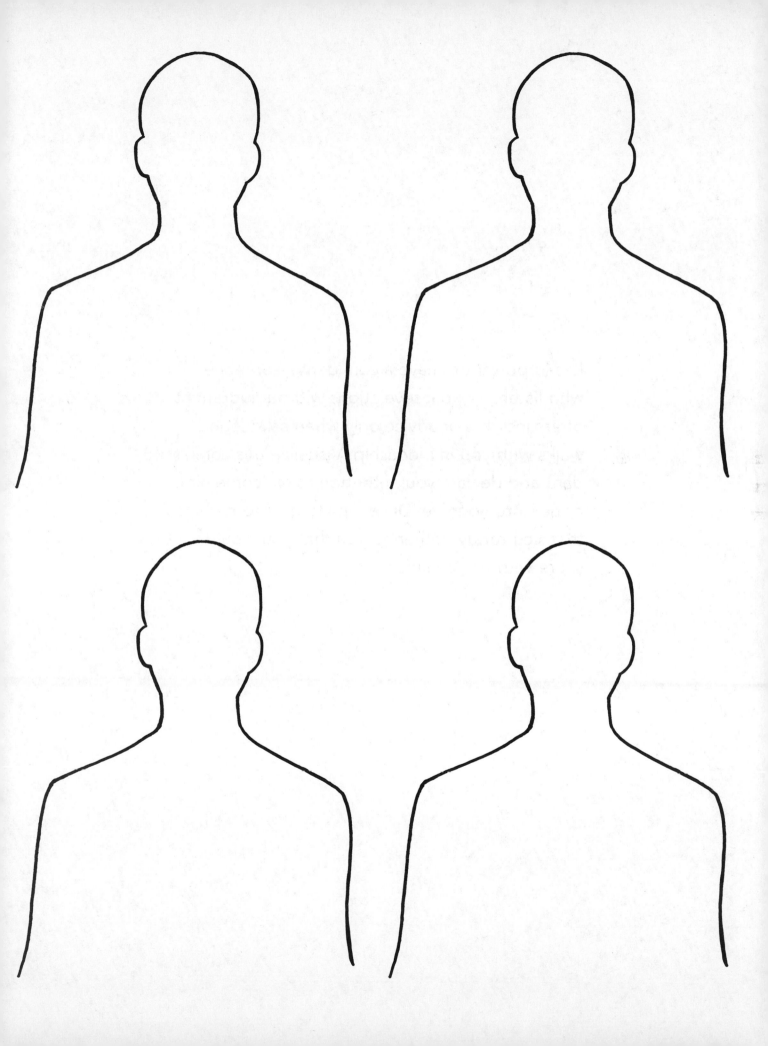

It is important to have a confidant—someone who listens to your revelations without judgment, offers insights or advice only when asked, and walks with you in friendship. Visualize this confidant and declare your intention to welcome him or her into your life. Draw a picture of something that's currently bothering you that you would share with this confidant.

MIDDLE-LEVEL DESIRES TO BUILD ON

Draw your new business cards. Use creative thinking to imagine you've already landed your dream job and are now passing out these business cards to everyone. Include the company logo and your new title. Form an intention to work there and rearrange your life to accommodate that job so it will manifest in accordance with your desire.

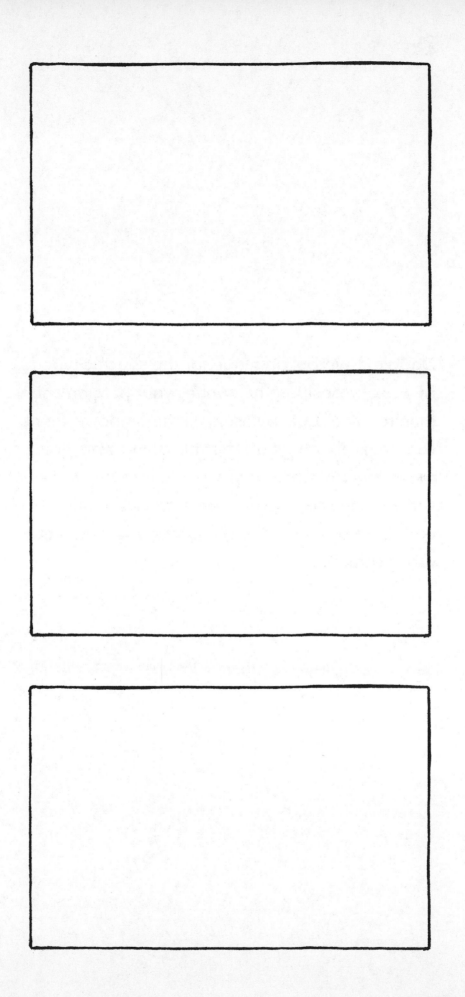

Doodle a symbol or image for the specific type of work or position that ignites your passion and manifest that goal by using all the empowerment tools available to you. After all, doing what you most love isn't really work, is it? Surround yourself with helpful people, contact a headhunter or employment service, and visualize yourself in that new position.

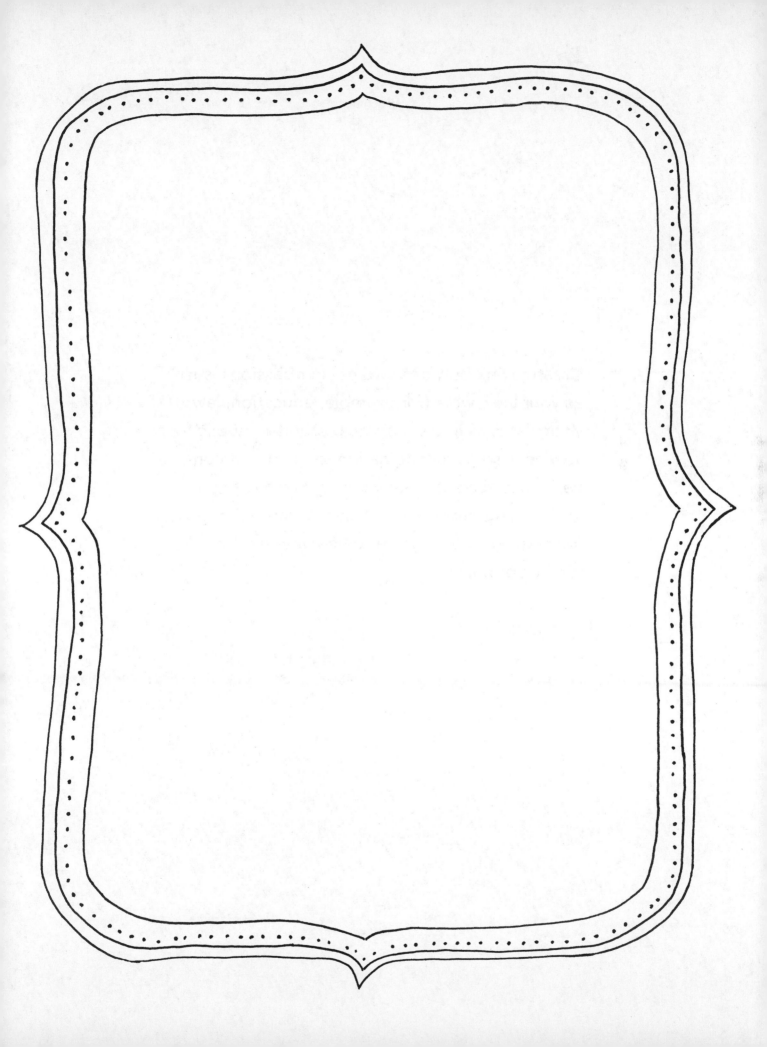

Create a link between two of your passions, such as your life's work (for example, education, law, or art) and your desire to help others in public service. Use your imagination to build that connection and create that working world with you in it, feeling happy and fulfilled. Draw an image near each link to represent the two passions you're combining.

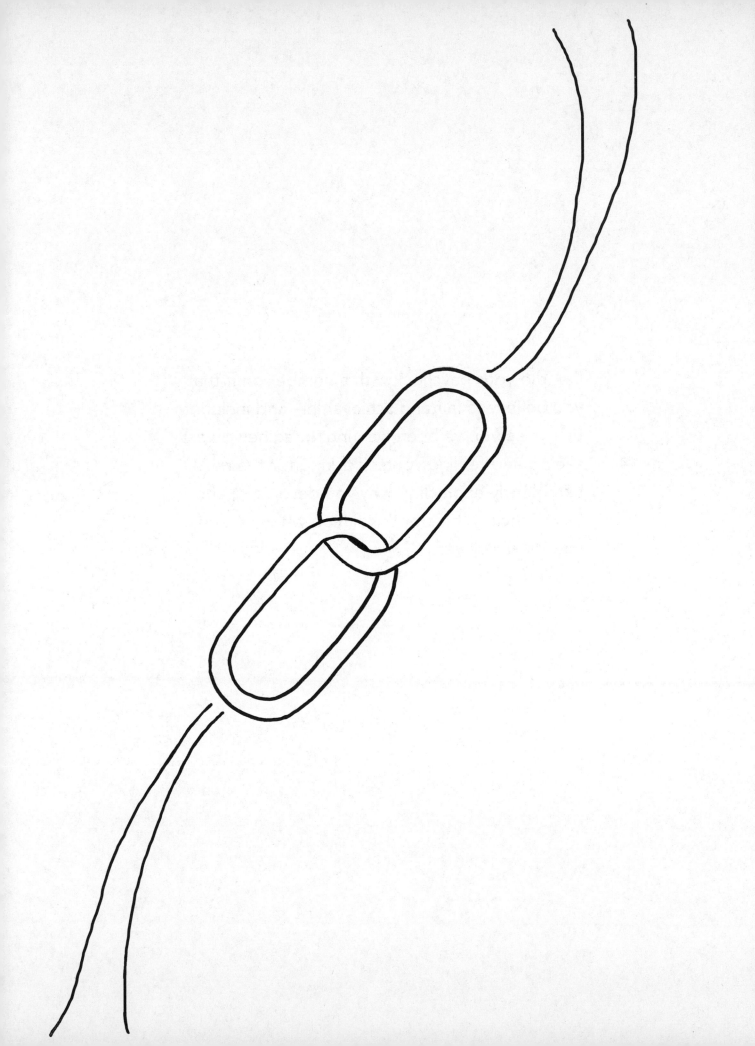

Doodle your paycheck with a number on it that you believe is fair and achievable—and includes that raise you've been wanting. Imagine you are seeing and feeling yourself asking for the raise, confidently explaining why you deserve it, and experiencing the emotional high when you hear your boss say yes.

In the empty frame, draw a musical instrument you've always wanted to play. Through the injection of your intention in the subtle field of possibilities, creative visualization, and actions in the world, attraction will draw that instrument into your orbit—and possibly the teacher and some music books, too.

Focus on the heartfelt desire to draw nearer to your life partner, perhaps to renew your relationship, or to face some difficult life challenge. Imagine the two of you forging a deeper, more loving emotional connection and being fully present to each other's needs and desires. Illustrate and write in the things that you two love to share.

Draw a representation of your spiritual beliefs or religion—maybe it's a mandala or religious icon. This image can serve as your point of departure into meditation, prayer, words, and actions that make your desires become your truths.

Make a doodle of a symbol sacred to you that will represent a holy site or place in the world that you dream of visiting, perhaps during a planned pilgrimage or just a vacation. Use your creative imagination to see yourself on the way, arriving, experiencing all the sensual details of that place, and feeling the emotional high.

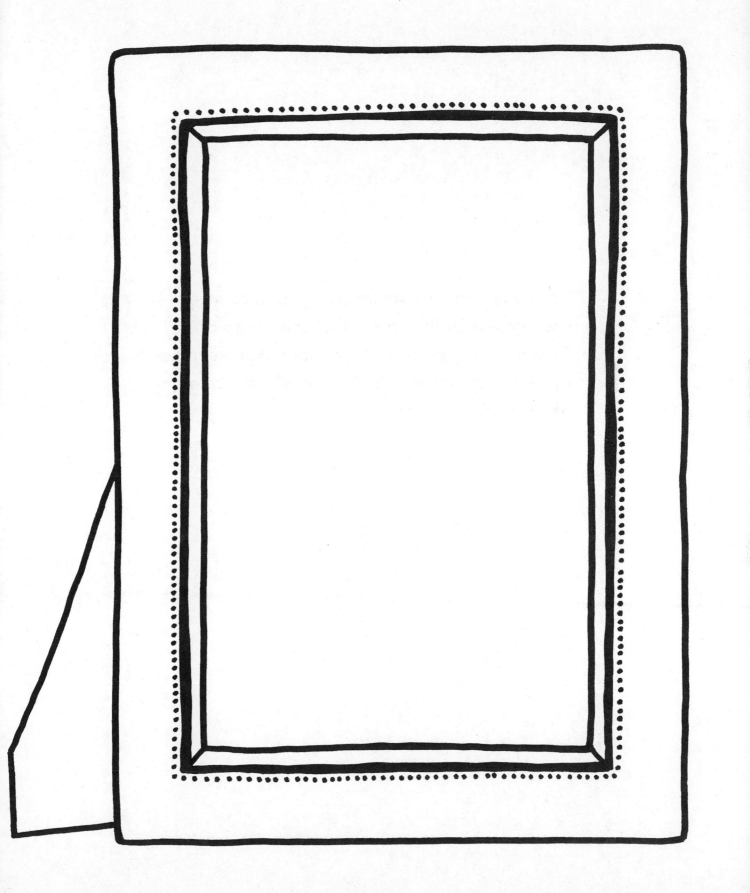

Draw you and your soulmate. What does he or she look like? What does he or she like to do? Creatively imagine your heart open and receptive to messages of love and see the world in terms of couples, yours among them.

Create a scene that depicts the vastness of nature in order to claim the abundance that is always available to you. You could draw a river flowing from a mountaintop to the sea to indicate your desire to live life fully present in each moment. Make time to daydream about the abundance already in your life, and what more you want access to—remember, your energized, positive thought and intention is what brings the blessings of abundance.

Sketch a beach chair and umbrella to symbolize your passion for having a house at the beach or more beach time. Let the image become a touchstone for creatively imagining life in that beach house, perhaps with family and friends, making all the more real your dream and intention.

Remember, you have the same amount of time in a twenty-four hour period as everyone else. Draw something that you would like to add to your daily routine that's specifically for you. To carve out more personal time, rethink your schedule and imagine ways to put your own priorities first. Give your plan a test run, and intend for a shift so that it can come.

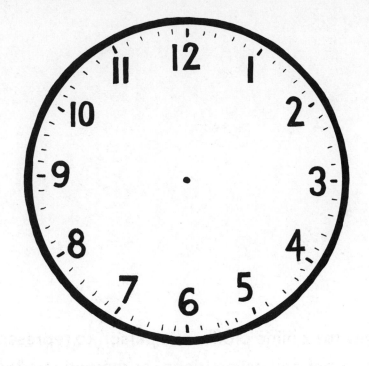

Draw the online profile of a person to represent a new penpal, online friend, or romantic partner whom you desire to attract. List the attributes you want the person to have and the role in your life he or she will fill. Be precise in what you want when visualizing or declaring intent, because what you create in your mind can happen online with a match as quick as a click.

What do you want right NOW? Use your creative imagination to manifest that desire in the present moment. Show yourself what you want right NOW by filling it in with words and doodles that represent your current want.

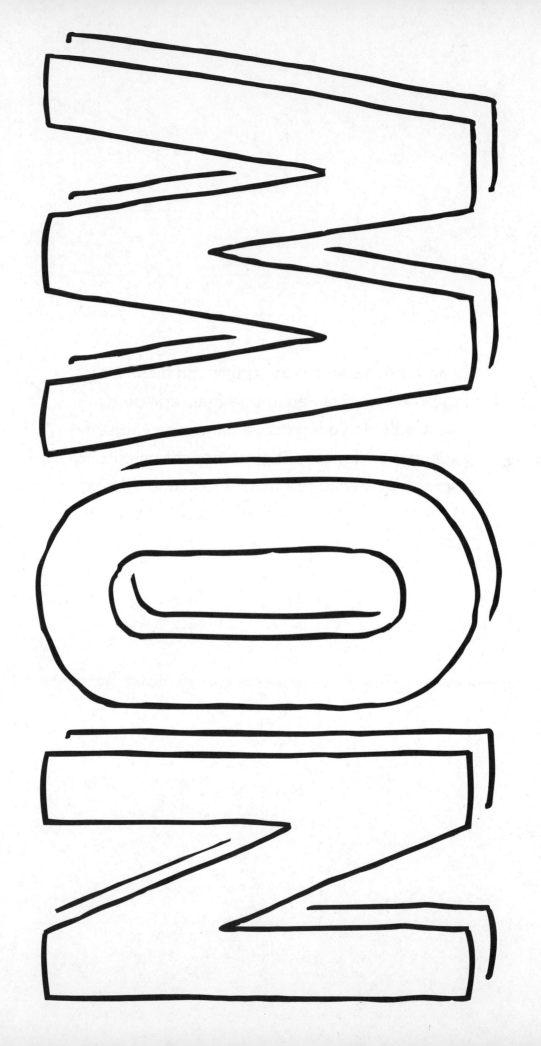

Imagine this sword cutting through a challenging problem. Draw an image that represents this hurdle. In your creative mind, see yourself as an expert fencer and problem solver, cutting through obstacles to get to a resolution. Next, make the intention, take the action, and get the result you desire.

Fill this vault with all types of currency and valuables to symbolize a desire to attract wealth. Visualize large-denomination bills, rare coins, gold bars, stocks and bonds, jewels, and more.

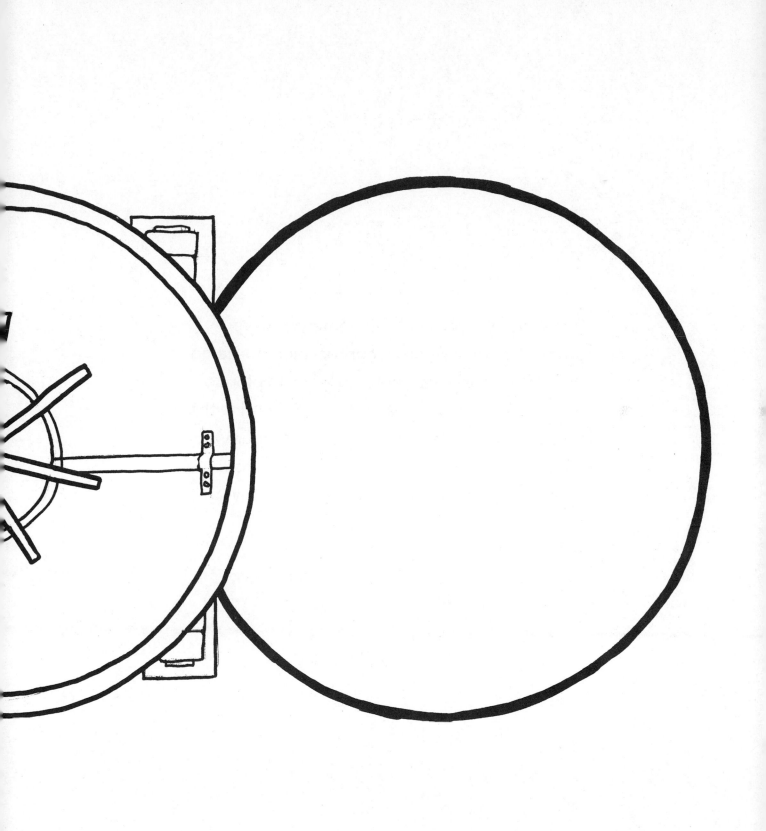

Draw the blueprints of the home you have always wanted. Visualize approaching it, seeing the exterior and entrance, and then exploring the physical space of each room as you visit the house, sign the papers, and move in. Your vision, intention, and will to have it ignite the unseen creative power and force for manifesting your dream.

Create an image of a large dinner, where family and friends gather around to enjoy food and drink. Use creative thoughts to imagine all the sensory details (see, hear, touch, taste, and smell) and let this meal act as a symbol for your aspiration to share great times with your friends and family.

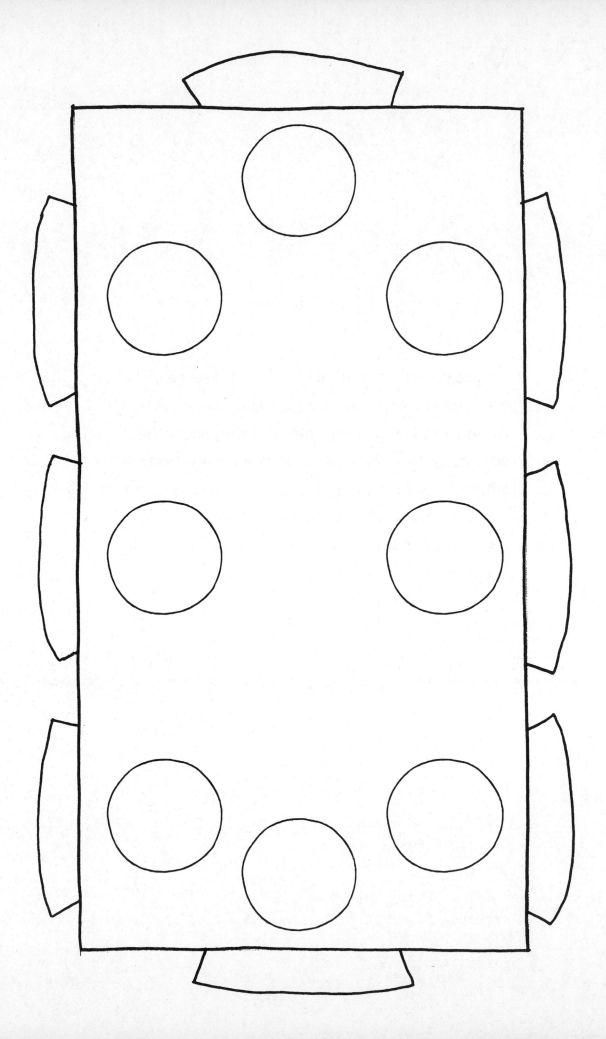

You can ease mental anguish and depression through movement. Unleash sublime joy and happiness by getting up and doing something active. Try and capture that movement on the page. Imagine you are dancing, running, or practicing yoga, and let your hand and mind wander, creating an abstract interpretation of your movement.

Being outside allows you to commune with nature and find peace. Create your own area out in the woods where you can spend some time alone. Fill in the space with your necessities—a tent, campfire, and so on—and imagine the feeling of peace this place will bring you.

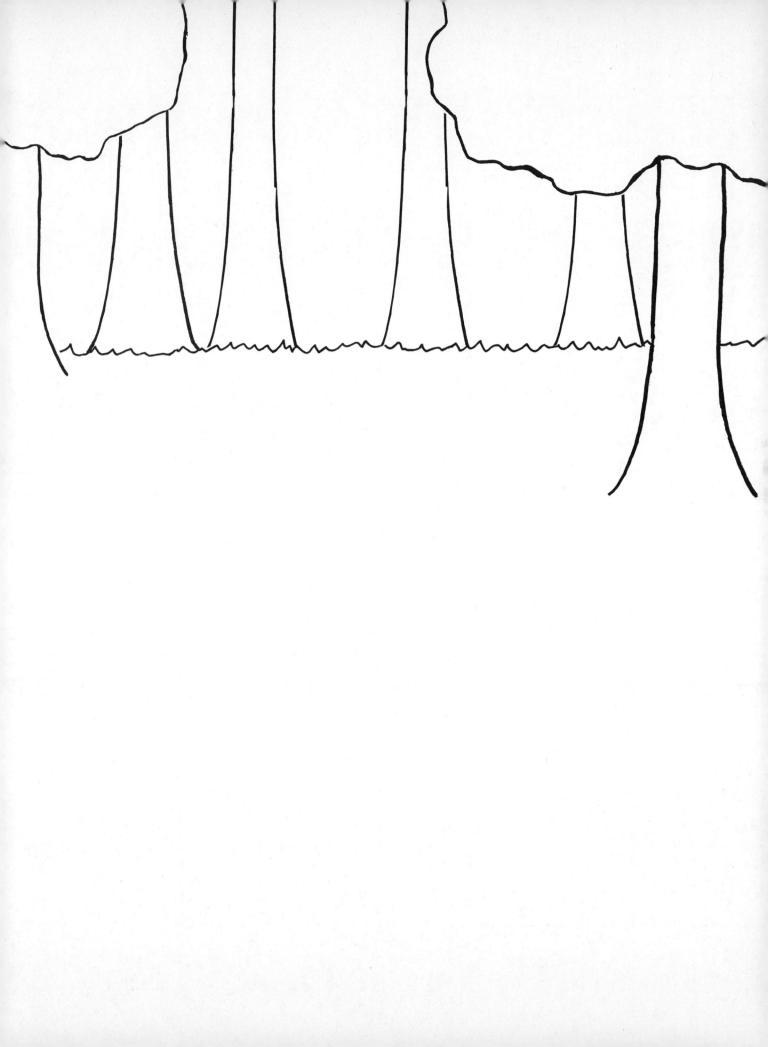

Sketch a beach house, cottage, or cabin to indicate that second house you've wanted. Make
it happen in your creative thoughts, visualize it,
take action (like visiting real estate agents in your
chosen time-away town or scanning real estate
websites) and make claim to your new home
away from home.

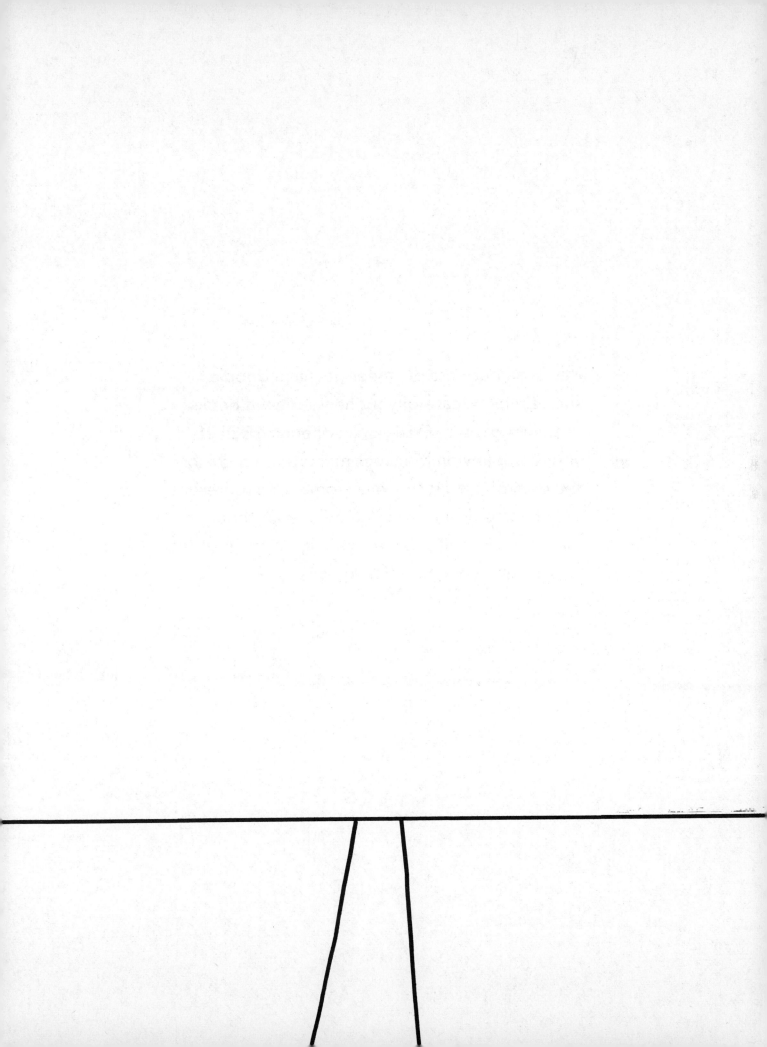

Render a business or career goal in a doodle, such as the release of your new series of books or paintings, the initial public offering (IPO) of your company on the stock market, or reaching the goal of 1 million new customers, to represent your heart's desire. The energy of your thoughts makes reality shift, so start envisioning that event and making your intention known.

Draw a banner for a charitable fundraiser you'll direct to raise money and awareness for a cause close to your heart. Show you are grateful for all the blessings in your life by helping those in need of assistance. See that banner in your creative thoughts, mull over the specifics in your mental theater, feel the message resonate in your heart, and proclaim to the world the necessity and worthwhileness of this enterprise to attract it.

Have you dreamed of starring in a movie? Create the movie poster for your film adventure. Play this dream in the cinema of your mind, visualizing the emotion within each scene.

Sketch out an invention that improves upon an ordinary tool for carpenters, cooks, car makers, or other field of endeavor. Let your doodle become an image for brainstorming and feel your excitement build as you see yourself developing, patenting, and marketing—then reaping the financial rewards for—your creative invention.

Give expression to your ideas for a room in your home that you dream of remodeling. Visualize the space. Draw a new design for that room, daydreaming the details until they are absolutely clear in your mind. Then, make a verbal intention to have that new look in the place so you will attract those changes.

Take a look at some websites and then doodle into expression a design for a site you desire to build for yourself, a friend, or a client (myriad templates available today make it easy). Through your creative imagining and then actually building your website, enjoy the sense of empowerment as you use it to promote your business, share a family tree and photo album, or establish an online business.

Doodle that boat you've dreamed of owning. Maybe it's a simple fishing boat or kayak, or something larger like a speedboat, cabin cruiser, or yacht. By fully imagining all the details with the powerful intention of acquiring it, you are establishing the attraction to pull in that boat. Get ready to claim it and name it.

Let your desire to spend more time on weekend trips push your pencil. Decide where you want to go for some much-needed fun time—be it wine country, an arboretum, on the water, or in fields where you pick your own fruit—and illustrate the destination. Check out the possibilities in your area then start visualizing daytripping and allow the universe to blow wind in your sails.

Doodle an entry from your bucket list. Tackling the items on your list one at a time, start the manifestation process by creatively imagining one item and then release your desire and intention to accomplish it. Let it go with the uncertainty of when or how it will manifest; just believe it will.

Draw a bird as if its freedom of flight might symbolize your desire to escape some difficult situation. Whether it's your demanding job, challenging marriage, or strict environment with rigid rules that hold you back, use your imagination to feel free in the present moment. You are a spirit, and you can create a nourishing tomorrow.

Doodle an oval picture frame featuring the name of someone you desire to honor or have your community honor with a park bench, a recreation center, a section of highway, or even a star in the night sky (to bear his or her name). Make your dream tangible through imagination, intention, and acts that demonstrate your commitment to manifesting this idea.

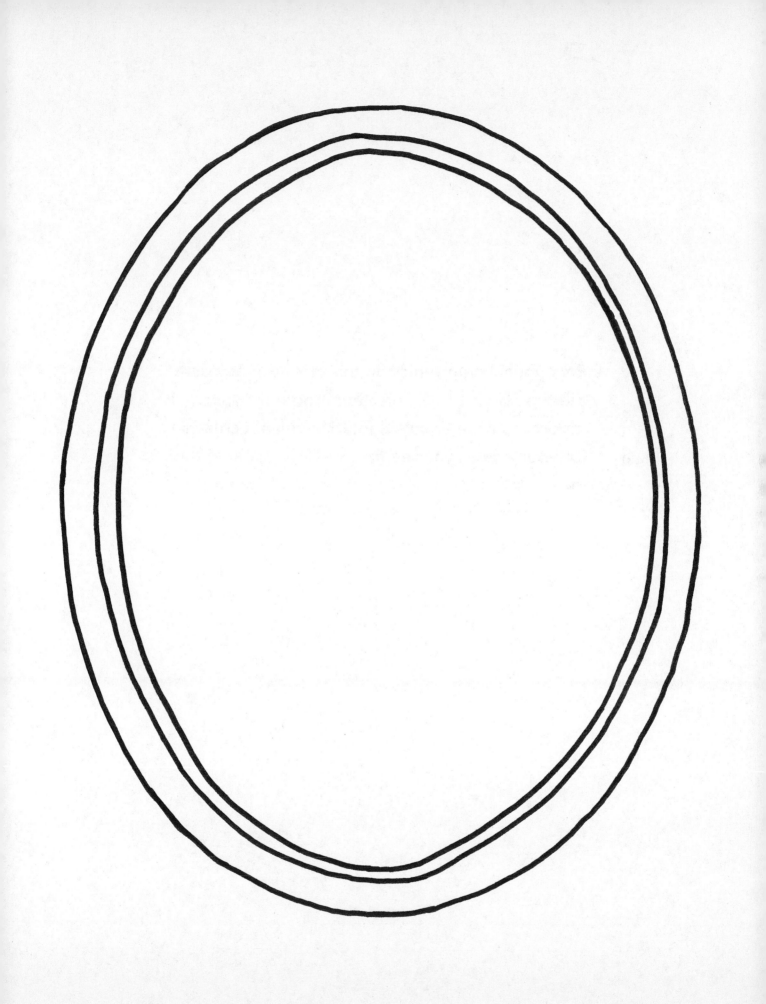

Park your dream vehicle in this driveway. Imagine the type of car, truck, or other mode of transportation you have always wanted to drive. Customize your ride as you see fit.

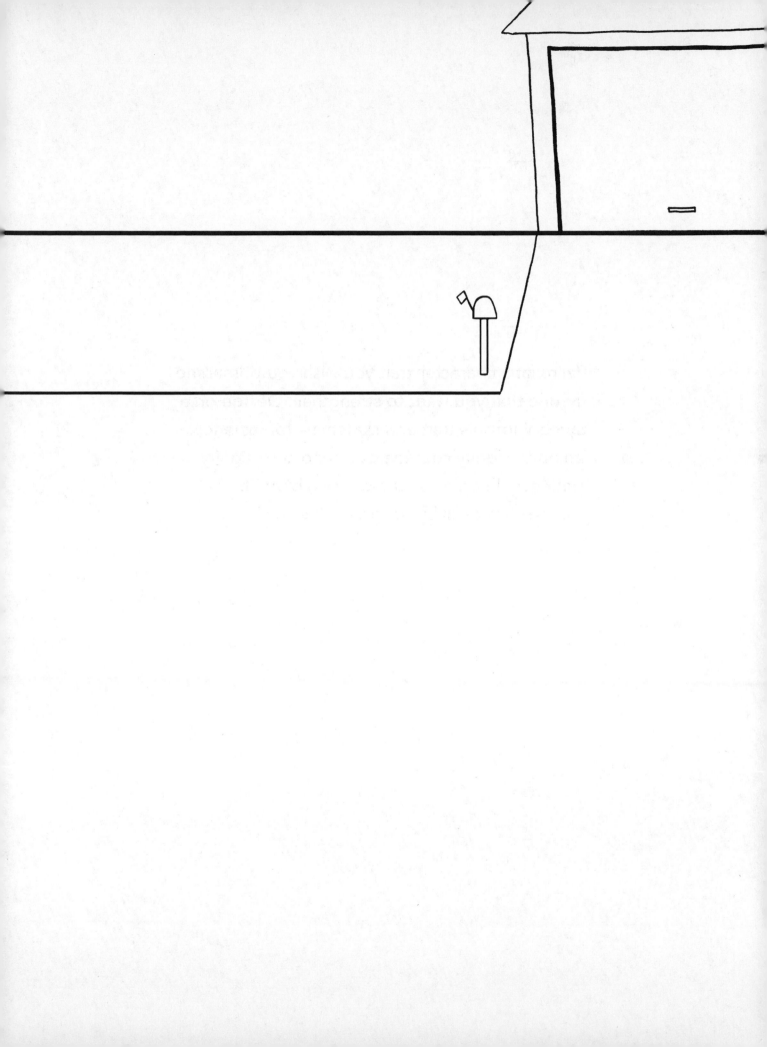

Think of a character trait you wish you possessed, or one that you want to strengthen. Decide on a symbol for this trait and sketch it—for instance, a lion to signify courage or a sundial to signify patience. Imagine all the positive benefits that this new trait will bring to your life.

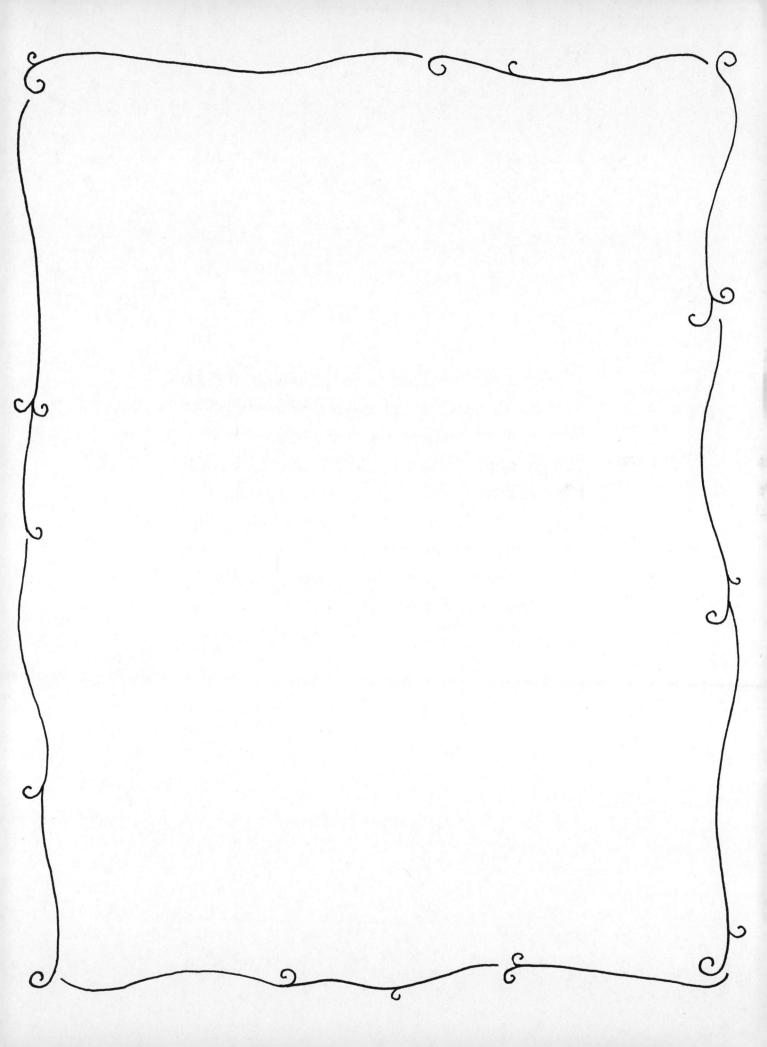

Now that you have practiced the power of drawing your desires through guided prompts, allow your own creativity to manifest whatever it is you are hoping to attract. These next few pages are blank canvases for your wants and wishes. Use your creative mind to visualize the tangibles and intangibles you wish to attain. Focus your thoughts, generate positive energy, and draw your dreams into reality.

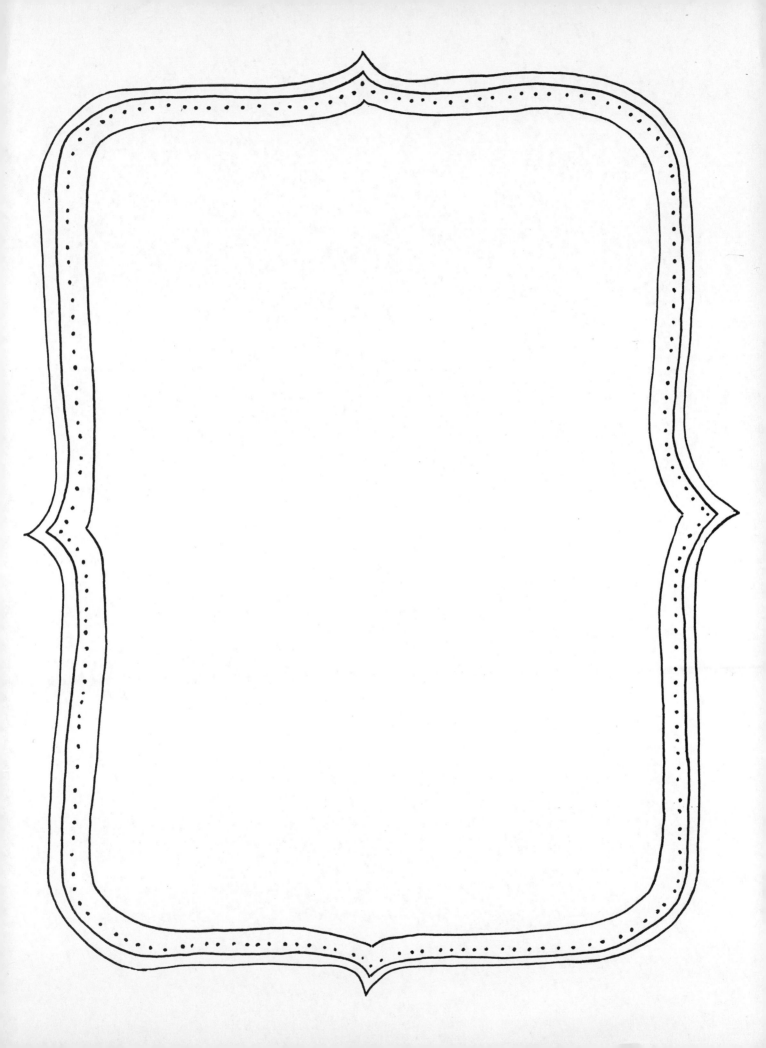